CONTINENTS

South America

Mary Virginia Fox

Heinemann Library
Chicago, Illinois

Designed by Depke Design
Printed in Hong Kong

05 04
10 9 8 7 6 5 4

Library of Congress Cataloging-in-Publication Data
Fox, Mary Virginia.
        South America / Mary Virginia Fox.
                p. cm. -- (Continents)
        Includes bibliographical references and index.
        ISBN 1-58810-002-2
        1. South America--Juvenile literature. 2. South
        America--Geography--Juvenile literature. I.Title. II. Continents
(Chicago, Ill.)
F2208.5 .F695 2001
980--dc21   00-011470

Acknowledgments
The publishers are grateful to the following for permission to reproduce copyright material: Earth Scenes/Fabio Colonbini, p. 5; Photo Edit/E. Zuckerman, p. 6; Earth Scenes/Breck P. Kent, pp. 9, 19; Tony Stone/Kevin Schafer, p. 11; Corbis/Adam Woolfitt, p. 13; Brian Vikander, p. 14; Animals Animals/Partridge, p. 15; Earth Scenes, p. 16; Tony Stone/Avenida Paulista, p. 20; DDB Stock Photo/ Robert Fried, p. 21; Peter Arnold/Jeff Greenberg, Inc., p. 23; Earth Scenes/Nigel J. H. Smith, p. 24; Earth Scenes/Michael Fogden, p. 25; Bruce Coleman/Timothy O'Keefe, Inc., p. 26; Tony Stone/Ary Diesendruck, p. 27; Photo Researchers/Georg Gerster, p. 28.

Every effort has been made to contact copyright holders of any material reproduced in this book. Any omissions will be rectified in subsequent printings if notice is given to the publisher.

Some words are shown in bold, **like this.**
You can find out what they mean by looking
in the glossary.

Contents

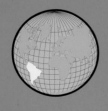

Where Is South America?

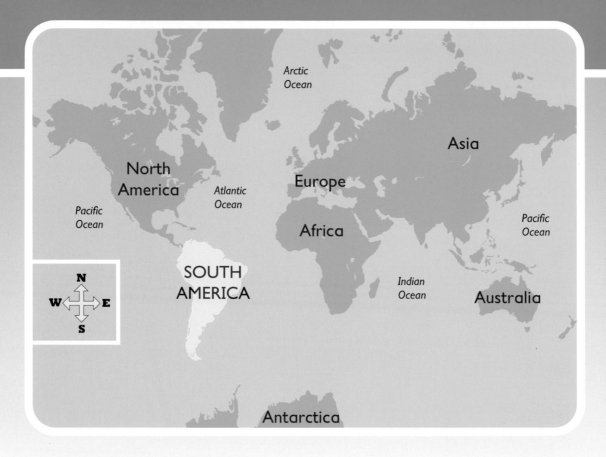

Arctic
Ocean

Asia

North
America

Europe

Atlantic
Ocean

Pacific
Ocean

Africa

Pacific
Ocean

N

W — E

S

SOUTH
AMERICA

Indian
Ocean

Australia

Antarctica

There are seven continents in the world. South
America is the fourth largest. Most of South
America is in the **Southern Hemisphere.**

Brazil

The Atlantic Ocean splashes South America's east coast. To the west is the Pacific Ocean.

Weather

Amazon River, Brazil

The **equator** crosses South America near its widest part. This area is the world's largest **rain forest**. It is hot and **humid**.

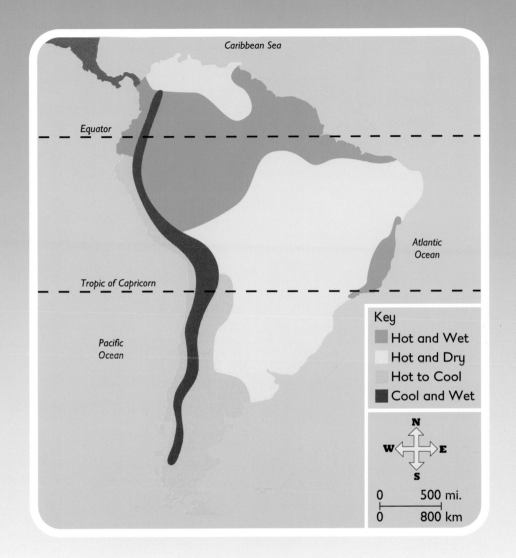

Caribbean Sea

Equator

Tropic of Capricorn

Pacific
Ocean

Atlantic
Ocean

Key
Hot and Wet
Hot and Dry
Hot to Cool
Cool and Wet

N
W   E
S

0   500 mi.
0   800 km

The tip of South America is very cold and windy.
It is closer to the continent of Antarctica, which is
the coldest area on Earth.

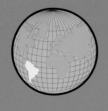# Mountains and Deserts

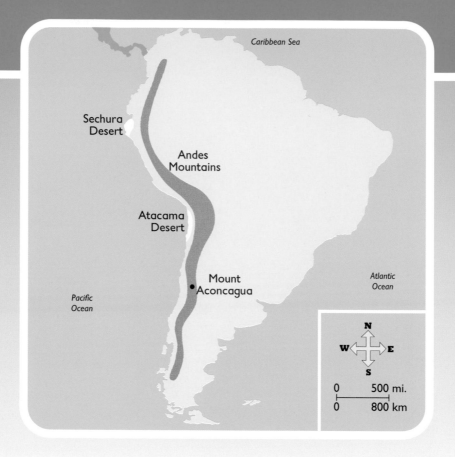

The Andes Mountains rise along the western **coast** of South America. The Andes are the longest mountain **range** on land in the world. The tallest mountain is Aconcagua.

Atacama Desert, Peru

Flat desert land stretches across South America on the west side of the Andes Mountains. Areas of grassland called *llanos* cover the northern center of the continent.

More water flows in the Amazon River than in any other river. It is the second longest river in the world.

Angel Falls, Venezuela

The Angel River drops almost a mile into a deep
gorge in the northeastern part of South America.
This is Angel Falls. It is the tallest waterfall in
the world.

Lakes

Caribbean Sea

Lake Guatavita

Lake Titicaca

Lake Poupó

Pacific
Ocean

Lake
Chiquita

Lake
Mirim

Atlantic
Ocean

Lake
Buenos
Aires

N
W   E
S

0   500 mi.
0   800 km

Lake Titicaca is high in the Andes Mountains.
This lake is so large that it warms the air around it.

Lake Guatavita, Colombia

Lake Guatavita is a round lake in the northern Andes Mountains. **Ancient** peoples thought this was where the sun was born.

Animals

Alpacas in Peru

High in the mountains, farmers raise llamas, *vicuñas,* and alpacas for their fine wool. These animals look like small camels. They are also used to carry heavy loads.

Anaconda

Anacondas are snakes that live in the jungles of
South America. They are one of the world's
largest snakes. Some can grow to be longer than
a soccer goal.

Plants

Rubber tree, Brazil

Rubber comes from the **sap** of rubber trees that grow in South America. Chewing gum is made from chicle, which comes from the sap of the sapodilla tree.

Cacao tree, Brazil

Chocolate is made from the seeds of the cacao tree. The cacao tree grows well in the **humid** forests of South America. The people of South America were among the first to make chocolate.

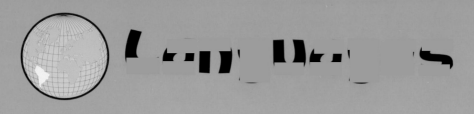

There are thirteen countries in South America. Most people speak Spanish or **Portuguese.** People from Europe explored South America hundreds of years ago. They brought their languages with them.

Yahua Indians, Peru

The first people to live in South America were
Indians. They had their own languages. Today,
only a few Indians in South America remember the
languages of their **ancestors**.

Cities

São Paulo, Brazil

São Paulo is on the southeastern **coast.** It is the largest city in South America. Large amounts of coffee were bought and sold in São Paulo. It became an important business city.

Santiago, Chile

Santiago sits below the Andes Mountains. Money made from **mines** made Santiago a wealthy city. The Biblioteca Nacional in Santiago is South America's largest library.

Quito, Ecuador

Quito is one of the highest cities in world. It sits on the side of a **volcano.** It is the oldest **capital city** in South America.

Rio de Janeiro is the busiest **port** in South America. Ships dock there from all over the world. This city is famous for its beautiful beaches and lively **festivals.**

Amazon River, Brazil

In the jungles of South America, most people live along rivers. Traveling by boat is the only way to get from one village to another. There are few roads.

Cuzco, Peru

High in the mountains, sheep and llama **herders** live in small houses built of clay bricks. It is cold there. Many people wear wool shawls called *ruanas* to keep warm.

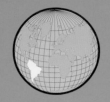

Machu Picchu, Peru

Long ago, Indians built a walled city called
Machu Picchu. It was hidden from the rest
of the world for hundreds of years.

Rio de Janeiro, Brazil

In Rio de Janeiro, a large statue of Jesus looks over the **harbor.** It can be seen from very far away.

Salt Mine Church, Colombia

In Colombia, a large salt **mine** has been made into a church. Even the statues have been carved out of salt.

Caribbean Sea

• Salt Mine Church
•Gold Museum

Machu
Picchu
•

Jesus Statue •

Pacific
Ocean

Atlantic
Ocean

N
W E
S

| 0 | 500 mi. |
| 0 | 800 km |

Many people come to see the Gold Museum in
Bogotá, Colombia. There are also **emerald**
mines near by.

1. South America has the world's largest rain forest—the Amazon.

2. The Atacama Desert in northern Chile is one of the driest places in the world.

3. Angel Falls has a longer drop than any other waterfall in the world (3,212 feet, 979 meters)

4. Many plants grow in South America and in no other continent.

5. The Amazon River rain forest has more kinds of plants than any other place in the world.

6. South America has some of the largest farms in the world.

7. Quito, Ecuador, lies almost two miles (three kilometers) above the Pacific Ocean.

8. The Andes Mountains are the world's longest mountain range above sea level (4,500 miles, 7,200 kilometers)

9. The hottest weather in South America is in Argentina's Gran Chaco, where the temperature reaches 110°F (43°C).

Glossary

ancestor one from whom an individual is descended

ancient something from a very long time ago

capital city city where government leaders work

coast land right next to the water

emeralds valuable green jewels

equator imaginary circle around the exact middle of the earth

festival time of celebration

gorge narrow or steep walled canyon

harbor safe place for ships and boats to stay

herder person who takes care of a group of animals

humid wet or containing water

mine hole in the earth from which valuable substances are taken

port place where ships load and unload cargo

rain forest thick forest that gets heavy rainfall all year

range line of connected mountains

sap liquid part of a plant

Southern Hemisphere half of the earth south of the equator

volcano hole in the earth from which hot, melted rock is thrown out

More Books to Read

Petersen, David. *South America.* Danbury, Conn.: Children's Press, 1998.

Sammis, Fran. *South America.* Tarrytown, N.Y.: Marshall Cavendish Corp., 1999.

Sayre, April Pulley. *South America.* Brookfield, Conn.: Twenty-First Century Books, Inc., 1999.

Index